HARD WALLET ORGA...

Hard Wallet Organizer: For Storing Cryptocurrency, Exchange Accounts and More

Published by: Encrypted Publishing Solutions, LLC.

Atlanta, Georgia, U.S.A.

Copyright ©2019 MARIO L. BUTLER. All rights reserved.

No part of this book may be reproduced in any form or by any mechanical means, including information storage and retrieval systems without permission in writing from the publisher/author, except by a reviewer who may quote passages in a review.

All images, logos, quotes, and trademarks included in this book are subject to use according to trademark and copyright laws of the United States of America.

BUTLER, MARIO L., Author
Hard Wallet Organizer
MARIO L. BUTLER

ISBN-13:   978-0-578-56562-0

HARD WALLET ORGANIZER

BUSINESS & ECONOMICS / E-Commerce / General

COMPUTERS / Electronic Commerce

Schools, companies, professional groups, clubs, and other organizations may qualify for special terms when ordering quantities of this title. For information, email:

 mario.butler@att.net

All rights reserved by MARIO L. BUTLER and ENCRYPTED PUBLISHING SOLUTIONS, LLC.

This book is printed in the United States of America.

HARD WALLET ORGANIZER

Purpose

This book was created for anyone who is involved in the world of cryptocurrency (digital assets). Before downloading any cryptocurrency wallet, signing up for an exchange account or creating a two-factor authentication on your smart phone, pad, or computer it is very important to have this book in front of you.

The purpose of this hard wallet organizer is for you to physically write your security keys, private keys, mnemonic phrases and 2 factor authentications so that you can always gain access to your cryptocurrency wallet and accounts. Storing this information online, taking photographs, and keeping it on a digital device puts you at risk of losing the information and being hacked by the best computer hackers in the world. Banks have even created devices stating they can store your keys and passwords but that is a service they will charge you for and you know we cannot trust banks with access to our funds.

This book will help you remain organized and accountable for all of your digital assets. Once you lose your security keys/mnemonic phrases YOU WILL LOSE ALL OF YOUR ASSETS AND NEVER BE ABLE TO ACCESS THEM AGAIN. The world of cryptocurrency will continue to expand, you will download multiple accounts to store and trade digital assets. I have included a glossary of terms as well for you to review so you can understand the terminology used on a daily basis in the crypto space.

Please keep this book in a safe place, preferably a safe, or safety deposit box.

This book is the first version and will have updated versions as more changes occur in the industry.

HARD WALLET ORGANIZER

How To Use This Book?

Step 1	In the event that someone steals your book please use a code name for the wallet that you are writing the key information for.
Step 2	Anytime you download a wallet to your smart phone or other device you will be assigned a public key and private key. The public key is used to share publicly with anyone you want to do a cryptographic transaction with. (Please write this code in the section provided) This information is also valuable because if it gets into the wrong hands there are Quantum computers that could use your public key to access funds as well.
Step 3	The private key/Mnemonic phrase is the code that you are to never share with anyone. If someone gains access to your private key then they can simply access your funds. (Please write this code in the section provided)
Step 4	Two-factor authentication-when setting up wallets on your device or exchange accounts on your computer they will ask you to setup this second layer of protection. This second layer of protection also comes with a security key or Mnemonic phrase (Please write this in the section provided).
Step 5	Remember to not leave large amounts of cryptocurrency sitting in hot wallets (online wallets) or any wallet on your smart device that is connected to the internet. Do not leave large amounts of cryptocurrency on exchanges because those funds can be hacked internally or externally.
Step 6	In the event that you lose your smart phone or other device make sure you have written down the correct code twice, there are enough pages in this book to write down your codes twice or three times.
Step 7	DO NOT LOSE THIS BOOK AND ENJOY GAINING WEALTH WITH CRYPTOCURRENCY.

Glossary of Terms

Keep in mind that there will be updated versions of this book and new terms will be added.

51% Attack

When more than half of the computing power of a cryptocurrency network is controlled by a single entity or group, this entity or group may issue conflicting transactions to harm the network, should they have the malicious intent to do so.

Address

Cryptocurrency addresses are used to send or receive transactions on the network. An address usually presents itself as a string of alphanumeric characters.

ASIC

Short form for 'Application Specific Integrated Circuit'. Often compared to GPUs, ASICs are specially made for mining and may offer significant power savings.

Bitcoin

Bitcoin is the first decentralized, open source cryptocurrency that runs on a global peer to peer network, without the need for middlemen and a centralized issuer.

Block

Blocks are packages of data that carry permanently recorded data on the blockchain network.

Blockchain

A blockchain is a shared ledger where transactions are permanently recorded by appending blocks. The blockchain serves as a historical record of all transactions that ever occurred, from the genesis block to the latest block, hence the name blockchain.

Block Explorer

Block explorer is an online tool to view all transactions, past and current, on the blockchain. They provide useful information such as network hash rate and transaction growth.

Block Height

The number of blocks connected on the blockchain.

Block Reward

A form of incentive for the miner who successfully calculated the hash in a block during mining. Verification of transactions on the blockchain generates new coins in the process, and the miner is rewarded a portion of those.

Central Ledger

A ledger maintained by a central agency.

Confirmation

The successful act of hashing a transaction and adding it to the blockchain.

Consensus

Consensus is achieved when all participants of the network agree on the validity of the transactions, ensuring that the ledgers are exact copies of each other.

Cryptocurrency

Also known as tokens, cryptocurrencies are representations of digital assets.

Cryptographic Hash Function

Cryptographic hashes produce a fixed-size and unique hash value from variable-size transaction input. The SHA-256 computational algorithm is an example of a cryptographic hash.

Dapp

A decentralized application (Dapp) is an application that is open source, operates autonomously, has its data stored on a blockchain, incentivised in the form of cryptographic tokens and operates on a protocol that shows proof of value.

DAO

Decentralized Autonomous Organizations can be thought of as corporations that run without any human intervention and surrender all forms of control to an incorruptible set of business rules.

Distributed Ledger

Distributed ledgers are ledgers in which data is stored across a network of decentralized nodes. A distributed ledger does not have to have its own currency and may be permissioned and private.

Distributed Network

A type of network where processing power and data are spread over the nodes rather than having a centralized data center.

Difficulty

This refers to how easily a data block of transaction information can be mined successfully.

Digital Signature

A digital code generated by public key encryption that is attached to an electronically transmitted document to verify its contents and the sender's identity.

Double Spending

Double spending occurs when a sum of money is spent more than once.

Ethereum

Ethereum is a blockchain-based decentralized platform for apps that run smart contracts, and is aimed at solving issues associated with censorship, fraud and third party interference.

EVM

The Ethereum Virtual Machine (EVM) is a Turing complete virtual machine that allows anyone to execute arbitrary EVM Byte Code. Every Ethereum node runs on the EVM to maintain consensus across the blockchain.

Fork

Forks create an alternate version of the blockchain, leaving two blockchains to run simultaneously on different parts of the network.

Genesis Block

The first or first few blocks of a blockchain.

Hard Fork

A type of fork that renders previously invalid transactions valid, and vice versa. This type of fork requires all nodes and users to upgrade to the latest version of the protocol software.

Hash

The act of performing a hash function on the output data. This is used for confirming coin transactions.

Hash Rate

Measurement of performance for the mining rig is expressed in hashes per second.

Hybrid PoS/PoW

A hybrid PoS/PoW allows for both Proof of Stake and Proof of Workas consensus distribution algorithms on the network. In this method, a balance between miners and voters (holders) may be achieved, creating a system of community-based governance by both insiders (holders) and outsiders (miners).

Mining

Mining is the act of validating blockchain transactions. The necessity of validation warrants an incentive for the miners, usually in the form of coins. In this cryptocurrency boom, mining can be a lucrative business when done properly. By choosing the most efficient and suitable hardware and mining target, mining can produce a stable form of passive income.

Multi-Signature

Multi-signature addresses provide an added layer of security by requiring more than one key to authorize a transaction.

Node

A copy of the ledger operated by a participant of the blockchain network.

Oracles

Oracles work as a bridge between the real world and the blockchain by providing data to the smart contracts.

Peer to Peer

Peer to Peer (P2P) refers to the decentralized interactions between two parties or more in a highly-interconnected network. Participants of a P2P network deal directly with each other through a single mediation point.

Public Address

A public address is the cryptographic hash of a public key. They act as email addresses that can be published anywhere, unlike private keys.

Private Key

A private key is a string of data that allows you to access the tokens in a specific wallet. They act as passwords that are kept hidden from anyone but the owner of the address.

Proof of Stake

A consensus distribution algorithm that rewards earnings based on the number of coins you own or hold. The more you invest in the coin, the more you gain by mining with this protocol.

Proof of Work

A consensus distribution algorithm that requires an active role in mining data blocks, often consuming resources, such as electricity. The more 'work' you do or the more computational power you provide, the more coins you are rewarded with.

Scrypt

Scrypt is a type of cryptographic algorithm and is used by Litecoin. Compared to SHA256, this is quicker as it does not use up as much processing time.

SHA-256

SHA-256 is a cryptographic algorithm used by cryptocurrencies such as Bitcoin. However, it uses a lot of computing power and processing time, forcing miners to form mining pools to capture gains.

Smart Contracts

Smart contracts encode business rules in a programmable language onto the blockchain and are enforced by the participants of the network.

Soft Fork

A soft fork differs from a hard fork in that only previously valid transactions are made invalid. Since old nodes recognize the new blocks as valid, a soft fork is essentially backward-compatible. This type of fork requires most miners upgrading in order to enforce, while a hard fork requires all nodes to agree on the new version.

Solidity

Solidity is Ethereum's programming language for developing smart contracts.

Testnet

A test blockchain used by developers to prevent expending assets on the main chain.

Transaction Block

A collection of transactions gathered into a block that can then be hashed and added to the blockchain.

Transaction Fee

All cryptocurrency transactions involve a small transaction fee. These transaction fees add up to account for the block reward that a miner receives when he successfully processes a block.

Turing Complete

Turing complete refers to the ability of a machine to perform calculations that any other programmable computer is capable of. An example of this is the Ethereum Virtual Machine (EVM).

Wallet

A file that houses private keys. It usually contains a software client which allows access to view and create transactions on a specific blockchain that the wallet is designed for.

HARD WALLET ORGANIZER

Cryptocurrency Wallet or Exchange/Code Name

Public Key

Private Key

Menomonic Key Phrase

Two Factor Authenticator Name/Code Name

Two Factor Authenticator Key

Notes

HARD WALLET ORGANIZER

Cryptocurrency Wallet or Exchange/Code Name

Public Key

Private Key

Menomonic Key Phrase

Two Factor Authenticator Name/Code Name

Two Factor Authenticator Key

Notes

HARD WALLET ORGANIZER

Cryptocurrency Wallet or Exchange/Code Name

Public Key

Private Key

Menomonic Key Phrase

Two Factor Authenticator Name/Code Name

Two Factor Authenticator Key

Notes

HARD WALLET ORGANIZER

Cryptocurrency Wallet or Exchange/Code Name

Public Key

Private Key

Menomonic Key Phrase

Two Factor Authenticator Name/Code Name

Two Factor Authenticator Key

Notes

ENCRYPTED PUBLISHING SOLUTIONS

HARD WALLET ORGANIZER

Cryptocurrency Wallet or Exchange/Code Name

Public Key

Private Key

Menomonic Key Phrase

Two Factor Authenticator Name/Code Name

Two Factor Authenticator Key

Notes

HARD WALLET ORGANIZER

Cryptocurrency Wallet or Exchange/Code Name

Public Key

Private Key

Menomonic Key Phrase

Two Factor Authenticator Name/Code Name

Two Factor Authenticator Key

Notes

ENCRYPTED PUBLISHING SOLUTIONS

HARD WALLET ORGANIZER

Cryptocurrency Wallet or Exchange/Code Name

Public Key

Private Key

Menomonic Key Phrase

Two Factor Authenticator Name/Code Name

Two Factor Authenticator Key

Notes

ENCRYPTED PUBLISHING SOLUTIONS

HARD WALLET ORGANIZER

Cryptocurrency Wallet or Exchange/Code Name

Public Key

Private Key

Menomonic Key Phrase

Two Factor Authenticator Name/Code Name

Two Factor Authenticator Key

Notes

ENCRYPTED PUBLISHING SOLUTIONS

HARD WALLET ORGANIZER

Cryptocurrency Wallet or Exchange/Code Name

Public Key

Private Key

Menomonic Key Phrase

Two Factor Authenticator Name/Code Name

Two Factor Authenticator Key

Notes

HARD WALLET ORGANIZER

Cryptocurrency Wallet or Exchange/Code Name

Public Key

Private Key

Menomonic Key Phrase

Two Factor Authenticator Name/Code Name

Two Factor Authenticator Key

Notes

ENCRYPTED PUBLISHING SOLUTIONS

HARD WALLET ORGANIZER

Cryptocurrency Wallet or Exchange/Code Name

Public Key

Private Key

Menomonic Key Phrase

Two Factor Authenticator Name/Code Name

Two Factor Authenticator Key

Notes

HARD WALLET ORGANIZER

Cryptocurrency Wallet or Exchange/Code Name

Public Key

Private Key

Menomonic Key Phrase

Two Factor Authenticator Name/Code Name

Two Factor Authenticator Key

Notes

ENCRYPTED PUBLISHING SOLUTIONS

HARD WALLET ORGANIZER

Cryptocurrency Wallet or Exchange/Code Name

Public Key

Private Key

Menomonic Key Phrase

Two Factor Authenticator Name/Code Name

Two Factor Authenticator Key

Notes

HARD WALLET ORGANIZER

Cryptocurrency Wallet or Exchange/Code Name

Public Key

Private Key

Menomonic Key Phrase

Two Factor Authenticator Name/Code Name

Two Factor Authenticator Key

Notes

HARD WALLET ORGANIZER

Cryptocurrency Wallet or Exchange/Code Name

Public Key

Private Key

Menomonic Key Phrase

Two Factor Authenticator Name/Code Name

Two Factor Authenticator Key

Notes

HARD WALLET ORGANIZER

Cryptocurrency Wallet or Exchange/Code Name

Public Key

Private Key

Menomonic Key Phrase

Two Factor Authenticator Name/Code Name

Two Factor Authenticator Key

Notes

ENCRYPTED PUBLISHING SOLUTIONS

HARD WALLET ORGANIZER

Cryptocurrency Wallet or Exchange/Code Name

Public Key

Private Key

Menomonic Key Phrase

Two Factor Authenticator Name/Code Name

Two Factor Authenticator Key

Notes

HARD WALLET ORGANIZER

Cryptocurrency Wallet or Exchange/Code Name

Public Key

Private Key

Menomonic Key Phrase

Two Factor Authenticator Name/Code Name

Two Factor Authenticator Key

Notes

HARD WALLET ORGANIZER

Cryptocurrency Wallet or Exchange/Code Name

Public Key

Private Key

Menomonic Key Phrase

Two Factor Authenticator Name/Code Name

Two Factor Authenticator Key

Notes

HARD WALLET ORGANIZER

Cryptocurrency Wallet or Exchange/Code Name

Public Key

Private Key

Menomonic Key Phrase

Two Factor Authenticator Name/Code Name

Two Factor Authenticator Key

Notes

ENCRYPTED PUBLISHING SOLUTIONS

HARD WALLET ORGANIZER

Cryptocurrency Wallet or Exchange/Code Name

Public Key

Private Key

Menomonic Key Phrase

Two Factor Authenticator Name/Code Name

Two Factor Authenticator Key

Notes

HARD WALLET ORGANIZER

Cryptocurrency Wallet or Exchange/Code Name

Public Key

Private Key

Menomonic Key Phrase

Two Factor Authenticator Name/Code Name

Two Factor Authenticator Key

Notes

HARD WALLET ORGANIZER

Cryptocurrency Wallet or Exchange/Code Name

Public Key

Private Key

Menomonic Key Phrase

Two Factor Authenticator Name/Code Name

Two Factor Authenticator Key

Notes

HARD WALLET ORGANIZER

Cryptocurrency Wallet or Exchange/Code Name

Public Key

Private Key

Menomonic Key Phrase

Two Factor Authenticator Name/Code Name

Two Factor Authenticator Key

Notes

HARD WALLET ORGANIZER

Cryptocurrency Wallet or Exchange/Code Name

Public Key

Private Key

Menomonic Key Phrase

Two Factor Authenticator Name/Code Name

Two Factor Authenticator Key

Notes

HARD WALLET ORGANIZER

Cryptocurrency Wallet or Exchange/Code Name

Public Key

Private Key

Menomonic Key Phrase

Two Factor Authenticator Name/Code Name

Two Factor Authenticator Key

Notes

ENCRYPTED PUBLISHING SOLUTIONS

HARD WALLET ORGANIZER

Cryptocurrency Wallet or Exchange/Code Name

Public Key

Private Key

Menomonic Key Phrase

Two Factor Authenticator Name/Code Name

Two Factor Authenticator Key

Notes

HARD WALLET ORGANIZER

Cryptocurrency Wallet or Exchange/Code Name

Public Key

Private Key

Menomonic Key Phrase

Two Factor Authenticator Name/Code Name

Two Factor Authenticator Key

Notes

ENCRYPTED PUBLISHING SOLUTIONS

HARD WALLET ORGANIZER

Cryptocurrency Wallet or Exchange/Code Name

Public Key

Private Key

Menomonic Key Phrase

Two Factor Authenticator Name/Code Name

Two Factor Authenticator Key

Notes

HARD WALLET ORGANIZER

Cryptocurrency Wallet or Exchange/Code Name

Public Key

Private Key

Menomonic Key Phrase

Two Factor Authenticator Name/Code Name

Two Factor Authenticator Key

Notes

HARD WALLET ORGANIZER

NOTES

HARD WALLET ORGANIZER

NOTES

HARD WALLET ORGANIZER

NOTES

HARD WALLET ORGANIZER

NOTES

HARD WALLET ORGANIZER

NOTES

HARD WALLET ORGANIZER

NOTES

HARD WALLET ORGANIZER

NOTES

HARD WALLET ORGANIZER

NOTES

HARD WALLET ORGANIZER

NOTES

HARD WALLET ORGANIZER

NOTES

HARD WALLET ORGANIZER

NOTES

HARD WALLET ORGANIZER

NOTES

HARD WALLET ORGANIZER

NOTES

HARD WALLET ORGANIZER

NOTES

HARD WALLET ORGANIZER

NOTES

HARD WALLET ORGANIZER

NOTES

HARD WALLET ORGANIZER

NOTES

HARD WALLET ORGANIZER

NOTES

HARD WALLET ORGANIZER

NOTES

HARD WALLET ORGANIZER

NOTES

CPSIA information can be obtained
at www.ICGtesting.com
Printed in the USA
LVHW061605200722
723979LV00011B/197